Uganda, United States and Europe: The Anti-Homosexual Law of 2014

M L Stevens

In Memory of David Kato

"First they came for the communists, and I did not speak out—
because I was not a communist;
Then they came for the socialists, and I did not speak out—
because I was not a socialist;
Then they came for the trade unionists, and I did not speak out—
because I was not a trade unionist;
Then they came for the Jews, and I did not speak out—
because I was not a Jew;
Then they came for me—
and there was no one left to speak out for me."

-Martin Niemoller

Introduction

Uganda is in a state of mass hysteria.

Whipped up by demagogic charlatans, the impoverished nation, facing herculean difficulties and teetering on the brink of an economic catastrophe, recently passed a law outlawing homosexuality. Not satisfied with their Anti-Sodomy Laws, the government will impose some of the harshest penalties in Africa on gay and lesbian citizens. The statute is sweeping and hastens a witch hunt.

By reading or loaning this book, you are a Ugandan criminal.

What should the West do to stand up for human rights? What will happen to the Ugandan gay population? Is there hope for repeal? These are moral and political questions that will be addressed, even if by the complicity of silence.

In Britain and the United States, Europe and Canada, the entire body politic must search their souls for a response.

For social liberals, a traditionally suppressed minority is being persecuted. As a result, Uganda is stepping backwards into a darker and more dangerous time.

For Conservatives, the law is a product of the super-state and they too must search for sensible policy. A collusion among the Ugandan Press, Church, Mosque and

Government is primed for a suppression of personal liberties. Ending foreign aid to Uganda might be a sensible option for the European and North American governments.

2 Background: Museveni Comes to Power

In 1979, Uganda was in ruins. The oppressive and mad dictator Idi Amin was deposed, but only after killing many Ugandans, establishing a brutal police state and setting back economic progress for decades. His rival, Milton Obote, assumed power and was nearly as horrible. Between the two of them, 600,000 Ugandans perished in a national bloodbath, many of them Christians. Obote held power until 1985[1] when Tito Okello Lutwa, an old associate of Obote and Amin's, ousted Obote.

---

[1] http://www.our-africa.org/uganda

On January 26, 1986, [2] Yoweri Museveni eventually took control of the government when a civil war brought him to power. Life gradually improved.

By 1996, Museveni and his allies forged a government from the various ethnic groups of Uganda. The new coalition established a human rights commission. An embryonic republic began to take shape as long ignored laws were enforced again. Local chiefdoms in remote rural areas revived with the federal government's blessing. Museveni's feat was notable; he managed to both strengthen the national identity of the country while providing greater sovereignty for its tribes.

---

[2]

http://www.britannica.com/EBchecked/topic/423934/Milton-Obote

In small steps, economic progress was evident. For better or worse, a fairly stable government was in place.

Unfortunately, Uganda gradually began sliding into dictatorship, as so many post-colonial states in Africa have done. Museveni won a national election in 1996, another in 2001 and then 2006. After "winning" another dubious election in 2011, he remains in power today.

The hard work that Ugandans put into the resurgence of the nation is long gone.[3]

---

[3] http://www.our-africa.org/uganda

3 Today: Uganda's Challenges

Uganda is a dangerous place facing a multitude of problems. Rampant crime, police corruption, erratic utilities services, backwards rural areas, disease and poor leadership are among them[4]

Ethnic disagreements lurk beneath the surface. Rioting erupted in 2009 [5] when supporters of a delegation from one of the rural areas of Uganda were arrested by the Kampala police. It was but one of many violent demonstrations over recent years.[6]

---

[4] http://www.state.gov/j/drl/rls/hrrpt/2010/af/154375.htm

[5] http://harpers.org/archive/2010/09/straight-mans-burden/4/

[6] http://www.hrw.org/news/2010/09/10/uganda-investigate-2009-kampala-riot-killings

The 30 million people of Uganda live a life of miserable poverty. Among the villages of Muslims and Christians that dot the country, about 25% of the country is illiterate, with the capital of Kampala having the best educated citizenry of all regions. It's a decent enough figure for sub-Saharan Africa, but urban literacy isn't enough to get the undeveloped country closer to modernity.

Unemployment is incredibly high. Trades such as carpentry and brick masonry, which have passed from one generation to the next, help provide food and extra amenities.

Some of the country is not electrified and trees are cut down for fuel and heating.[7]

---

[7] http://www.our-africa.org/uganda

Coffee is currently the nation's economic lifeline. 1 in 4 Ugandans derive some income from exporting java. The bitter brew brings in more than 250 million dollars per year. While coffee is a fine source of revenue, it also makes the country vulnerable to the divine caprice of a bad harvest. The recent discovery of oil in Uganda is a potential economic boom. However, if mismanaged, it will not be of benefit to the masses.

European and North American aid accounts for roughly 15% of national wealth.

The rate of deforestation is alarming. In the last 20 years, 66% of Uganda's forests have been cut down. At this rate, Uganda will share the same fate as Haiti, where the lack of landscaping now routinely causes flooding when heavy rain falls. Coupled with poverty and lack of adequate shelter, Uganda will fall into an international abyss *unless these problems become priorities*. [8]

Many homes are cheap wooden clapboard shelters.

Before the international outrage about the notorious anti-gay law, Uganda was already on slippery international footing as one of the worst offenders of illegal ivory trading in the world.[9]

More than 25% of Uganda's population is malnourished. The people have land available but there is little in the way of producing bumper crops to feed the nation. Things that are taken for granted

---

[8]

http://www.theguardian.com/society/katineblog/2009/jun/25/uganda-deforestation

[9] http://www.bbc.com/news/world-africa-14112446

in Britain and the United States, such as fertilizer, crop rotation and other means of farm production for the population are not well used in Uganda.

This is a young country and children's work on hardscrabble farms is often vital for a family to scratch out sustenance.[10] As a time tested universal truth, hunger and poor nutrition always take a greater toll on the young and the elderly. Uganda is no exception.[11]

Much of the rural population must survive on 75p - £1.50 or $1.25 daily.

As a pathetically burdened country, their priorities shouldn't be punishing people for who they are. In the short summation you are about to read, you will see how

---

[10] http://www.our-africa.org/uganda

[11] http://www.unicef.org/infobycountry/uganda_69289.html

the politicians, press and a few religious figures in Uganda have put their people on a path of destruction.

The hysteria that has been whipped up in Uganda against gay and lesbian citizens is disgraceful.[12]

To understand the roots of the anti-homosexual law recently passed, it is especially helpful to focus on the religious character that defines Uganda's culture.

---

[12] http://www.our-africa.org/uganda

4The Religious Culture of Uganda

Ugandans are a religious people.

Christians make up about 85% of the faithful, with Catholics being the largest group, followed by various Protestant sects (Anglican, Pentecostal, etc.). Religious practices among rural people are often charismatic, featuring joyous singing and dancing. Urbanites are generally Episcopal or Catholic.

Muslims constitute around 12% of the total population and are overwhelmingly Sunni. When Idi Amin suddenly expelled the vast Indian community in the 70's, most of the remnants left behind practiced Islam.

The daily pulse and vitality of the people's religion is easily demonstrated by official Ugandan holidays. Five are religious dates.[13]

Uganda's religious freedom is commendable and they have set, for the most part, good examples to other developing nations for interfaith pluralism. Among the more than 50 African nations, Muslims and Christians live together more harmoniously in Uganda than in most other nations on the continent. [14] However, this isn't always the case. As late as 2011, there have been religious riots between Muslims and Christians and within the Ugandan Muslim community.[15]

---

[13] http://www.state.gov/j/drl/rls/irf/2009/127261.htm

[14] http://www.folkways.si.edu/delicious-peace-coffee-music-and-interfaith-harmony-in-uganda/world/album/smithsonian

[15] http://mobile.monitor.co.ug/Life/-/1055104/1196860/-/format/xhtml/-/35mua5z/-/index.html

Politically speaking, today's Ugandan leadership has taken the asset of religious freedom and turned it into a debt.

Cynical observers see a law set up to distract the people from a failed government. It is better, perhaps, to talk about Homosexuals "recruiting" children than it is to address the severe poverty that affects them. It is a problem the Ugandan government seems unable to address. [16]

In the tradition of both Ugandan Islam and Christianity, homosexuality is regarded as an unspeakable sin. This brand of religious thinking is perfectly used to manipulate and distract the people.

---

[16] http://www.our-africa.org/uganda

5 The Anti-Homosexuality Bill, 2007-2012

Historically, Anti-Gay laws are not unusual in Uganda.[17]

Ugandan law discriminated against gays well before 2009, when post-colonial anti-gay laws were enacted. Human Rights Watch claims that people who were arrested under the old provisions were sometimes tortured.[18]

Furthermore, Uganda is not the sole African country with anti-sodomy laws on

---

[17]http://www.amnesty.org.uk/lgbti-lgbt-gay-human-rights-law-africa-uganda-kenya-nigeria-cameroon#.UxMbFRGPLIV

[18] http://www.hrw.org/en/news/2009/10/15/uganda-anti-homosexuality-bill-threatens-liberties-and-human-rights-defenders

their books. The continent has the most restrictive laws, taken as a whole, in the world. [19]

The origins of the Ugandan anti-gay bill started its long journey into becoming law when the popular, rabidly anti-gay minister Martin Ssempa held a political rally in 2007. At the gathering, he harped on the theme of the West interfering in Ugandan affairs.[20] This became a continuous routine. Ssempa used a typical quote in 2011 "We as religious leaders and civil society are distressed that the Anti-Homosexuality Bill is being deliberately killed largely by the undemocratic threats of Western

---

[19] http://www.pambazuka.org/en/category/features/90729

[20] http://news.bbc.co.uk/2/hi/africa/6957336.stm

nations," and repeating the same kinds of statements ad nauseam. [21]

By 2009, Ssempa was using an offensive hard core pornographic film, touring the country and painting the movie as an example of gay behavior. He became a kind of national court jester, delivering his buffoonish punch line "They eat de poo poo" as he stirred up angry crowds.[22]

Among other absurdities, Ssempa proposes "treatment facilities" for gays.[23]

Ssempa's prior statements about his fear of Western meddling in Ugandan affairs

---

[21] http://www.advocate.com/news/daily-news/2011/05/06/uganda-antigay-bill-going-forward

[22] http://www.reuters.com/article/2011/05/13/ozatp-uganda-gaybill-idAFJOE74C0HP20110513

[23]

http://www.nytimes.com/reuters/2014/03/09/world/africa/09reuters-uganda-gays.html?hp

are ironic, considering the long and well financed training he received in the United States by fringe evangelicals.[24] Ssempa is but one hypocrite among many in the leadership of Uganda.

The government must have the same label of hypocrite. Consider the fact that Uganda interfered in the Congo, sending troops into the middle of one of the bloodiest (and largely unnoticed by the West) wars of the 20th Century.[25]

When Martin Ssempa travelled around the United States in 2009, he caused a great deal of confusion among the American Christian Right. Rick Warren, pastor of the Saddleback Church in La Forest, California, initially welcomed

---

[24] http://www.christianitytoday.com/ct/2013/may-web-only/god-loves-uganda.html

Ssempa as a guest speaker. A short time later, Warren publicly spoke against the bill. [26]

The break was dramatic and public with Ssempa criticizing Warren for not speaking out against Homosexuality. After the break, Ssempa penned a public letter to Warren, criticizing him. [27]

Ssempa's advocacy of violence against the Ugandan LGBT community and his attempts to minimalize their status as humans makes him a candidate for the most reprehensible of the witch hunters in this tale.[28]

---

[26] http://abcnews.go.com/blogs/headlines/2009/12/africas-culture-war-the-fight-over-ugandas-antigay-bill/

[27] http://rhrealitycheck.org/article/2009/12/19/updated-martin-ssempa-responds-rick-warren-ugandas-homosexuality-bill/

[28] http://www.huffingtonpost.com/roger-ross-williams/god-loves-uganda_b_3520057.html

In March of 2009, a fringe American religious organization appeared in Uganda and staged a conference under the guise of defending the family. Three Americans, Stephen Langa, Scott Lively and Dan Schmierer of the ex-gay group Exodus International, arrived in Kampala to host the seminars. The group proclaimed the popular Ugandan idea that homosexuals were trying to take over the world. Ugandan police, citizens, teachers and government officials attended the meeting.[29] Lively, among the three, is often cited as having the most influence in Uganda.[30] He, with his co-author Kevin Abrams, wrote *The Pink*

---

[29] http://www.bbc.com/news/world-africa-14112446

[30] http://www.counterpunch.org/2014/03/07/yoweri-museveni-and-reconstruction-of-homophobic-colonial-legacy-in-africa/#_edn3

Swastika, said to blame Hitler's rise on homosexuals.

It is a strange book that weaves a fanciful yarn that gay men and women, in fact, were the heart of the Nazi movement.[31]

Lively's 2009 trip began with a meeting of 50 Ugandan Christian lawyers. Shortly thereafter, he addressed the national parliament.

By the end of the week, the three Americans had addressed thousands of Ugandans at Universities and churches. Lively made his way onto Ugandan television to accuse UNICEF of engaging in an attempt to indoctrinate Ugandan children into a gay lifestyle.

---

[31]http://www.splcenter.org/get-informed/intelligence-report/browse-all-issues/2005/spring/holy-war/making-myths

As extreme as Dr Lively appears to be, particularly irritating the British and American left, he felt afterwards that the law went too far. He believed the law should have been directed primarily at Child Sexual molestation.[32] Though he expressed reservations, Lively help set the table for the law, whether he changed his mind or not.

Once the bill picked up momentum, the tabloid Ugandan Press joined the pack.

The *Observer* printed handy tips for spotting homosexuals in 2009.[33]

---

[32]

http://www.defendthefamily.com/pfrc/archives.php?id=2345952

[33]

http://www.cnn.com/2009/WORLD/africa/12/08/uganda.anti.gay.bill/index.html?iref=allsearch

The wheels were in motion for the law to pass.

A member of the Ugandan Parliament, David Bahati, wrote the bill.[34] He had been mulling the idea over for a year by the time it was filed.[35]

In American domestic politics, Bahati might be compared to George Wallace or Joe McCarthy.

The MP is just as popular as either man was in his heyday. Bahati isn't stupid. He speaks three languages and has close ties with other government officials and businessmen from Uganda, developed through sophisticated politics.

---

[34] http://news.bbc.co.uk/2/hi/8412962.stm

[35] http://www.today.com/id/34362943/ns/msnbc_tv-rachel_maddow_show/#.UycBJBPD9y0

He was educated in Britain, the United States and Uganda, after a difficult childhood, in which he lost his parents. He emerged as an accountant in adulthood. A religious experience made him feel God was calling him to become involved with politics. During part of his time in the U.S., he mingled with various Right Wing think tank leaders, picking up methods and practices for use in Ugandan politics. [36]

His anti-gay law was formally introduced in the Ugandan Parliament in October[37]

---

[36] http://harpers.org/archive/2010/09/straight-mans-burden/4/

[37] http://harpers.org/archive/2010/09/straight-mans-burden/

of 2009[38], and the matter quickly gained attention in the West.[39]

The United States government began protesting the bill immediately, when Secretary of State Hillary Clinton spoke against the law, declaring that any "law should not become an instrument of oppression."[40]

Cables from the US mission in December of 2009 sounded an alarm about Ssempa and Bahati's activities.

"Bahati, [James Nsaba, Cabinet Member] Buturo, and particularly Ssempa's ability to channel popular anger over Uganda's

---

[38] http://www.publiceye.org/magazine/v24n4/us-christian-right-attack-on-gays-in-africa.html#

[39] http://edition.cnn.com/2014/02/24/world/africa/uganda-anti-gay-bill/

[40] http://abcnews.go.com/blogs/headlines/2009/12/africas-culture-war-the-fight-over-ugandas-antigay-bill/

socio-political failings into violent hatred of a previously unpopular but tolerated minority is chilling," read one early message.

Weeks earlier, David Kato, who will be discussed later, testified at a UN sponsored meeting in Uganda about the law. His speech was interrupted by endless laughing and jeers from Ugandan Government officials. [41]

In 2010, the Ugandan *Rolling Stone* (not affiliated with the American Magazine) set a precedent by publishing an article identifying 100 people as being gay. Included in photos were yellow strips with instructions to "hang them." It was proof of collusion with the government

---

[41]

http://www.theguardian.com/world/2011/feb/17/wikileaks-cables-gay-rights-uganda

came when Editor Giles Muhame, admitted the reason for the list was to have them arrested. [42]

In that climate, the bill moved along into the next year.

By 2010, Western governments increased pressure to fight the bill. Sweden and Britain led the way, stating that they would end the $50m (£31m) of annual aid they give to Uganda if the measure passed.

Facing a public relations disaster and the potential loss of international aid, Parliament speaker Edward Ssekandi disposed of the law through parliamentary procedure in 2010.

---

[42]

http://edition.cnn.com/2010/WORLD/africa/10/20/uganda.g ay.list/index.html

Ssekandi had been forewarned about the potential loss of revenue. He told a Christian audience as much in December of 2009 when he admitted the West was communicating to him that aid would be cut off if the bill became law. [43]

As the bill was resuscitated repeatedly through the next 3 years, British Prime Minister David Cameron began discussing aid restriction again in 2011. Britain gives an annual aid package of £70 million. [44] Once Britain and the EU announced that future aid to Uganda would be imperiled by such a law, the idea died for a time.[45]

---

[43] http://www.monitor.co.ug/News/National/-/688334/831784/-/wgnkjp/-/index.html

[44] http://www.onislam.net/english/news/africa/469431-uganda-muslims-laud-anti-gay-bill.html

[45] http://edition.cnn.com/2014/02/24/world/africa/uganda-anti-gay-bill/

Influential religious leaders in Uganda took up the cause of working to get the bill passed, such as Anglican Archbishop Henry Orombi of Uganda. [46]

As the next two years passed, the worst part of the law, the death penalty, was removed.

In October, British Prime Minister David Cameron stuck to his guns and continued warning Uganda that if such laws were passed, British aid might quickly be slashed or cut entirely.[47]

The bulk of the fight came from within Uganda.

---

[46] http://abcnews.go.com/blogs/headlines/2009/12/africas-culture-war-the-fight-over-ugandas-antigay-bill/

[47]http://www.dailymail.co.uk/news/article-2046965/Well-cut-aid-persecute-gays-Britain-warns-African-nations.html?ito=feeds-newsxml

Many citizens showed great courage by speaking out against the law.

Gay Rights activists like Bishop Christopher Senyonjo worked within Uganda, battling bravely, attempting to use the world's outrage to fight the law. [48]

The 78 year old bishop was educated in the United States in the early 60's, during the time of the flowering of African Independence. He returned to Africa and became the Bishop of the Anglican Diocese of Western Uganda, serving in that post for 24 years.

He met gay and lesbian youth and began to learn about their lives in the early part of the 21st century.

---

[48] http://www.reuters.com/article/2011/05/13/ozatp-uganda-gaybill-idAFJOE74C0HP20110513

Afterwards, his message became "If you are gay or lesbian, God made you and loves you that way, and you should accept yourselves."

It was a surprising message from an elderly clergyman and it gained him respect throughout the world. He spoke against the law for the entire time it was debated and amended. [49]

The aforementioned David Kato, was "outed" by one of the yellow tabloids that are sold in Uganda. He died by being beaten to death with a hammer.[50]

David Kato grew up in a socially conservative home and was brought up

---

[49]

http://www.religiondispatches.org/archive/sexandgender/2698/expelled_ugandan_bishop_ministers_to_lgbt

[50] http://www.reuters.com/article/2011/05/13/ozatp-uganda-gaybill-idAFJOE74C0HP20110513

with his family's mainstream African view that homosexuality was wrong. He left Uganda and was educated in South Africa, returning and becoming a school teacher for a time. At the time of his murder, he was the de facto national leader of the Ugandan LGBT community.

It is still unclear, five years later, whether the murder was a hate crime or if another motive compelled the murderer to kill him. [51]

Even Dan Schmierer, one of the three US evangelical who came to Uganda in 2009, was horrified to learn of Kato's murder.[52]

---

[51]

http://www.nytimes.com/2011/01/28/world/africa/28uganda.html?_r=0

[52]

http://www.nytimes.com/2011/01/28/world/africa/28uganda.html?_r=0

Other brave souls carried on.

Kasha Jacqueline Nabagesera, a lesbian activist in Uganda, was honored by Amnesty International for her appearances on Ugandan TV and her various press interactions. Originally an accountant, she changed careers and traveled to Massachusetts, receiving training at a liberal think tank (Human Rights Education Associates) along the lines of Amnesty International.[53]

She received several awards for her work in Uganda. Among them is The Martin Ennals Award for Human Rights Defenders. It is named after the late

---

[53]

http://www.frontlinedefenders.org/KashaJacquelineNabagesera

British lawyer who became the first head of the human rights organization.[54]

She acknowledged, not long after David Kato's murder, that she was forced to move frequently from place to place to survive.

There were courageous Christian leaders in Uganda spoke out against the bill, believing it to be a misuse of God's message of love for all of his children. Dr. Kapya Kaoma and Bishop Christopher Senyonjo bravely put their necks and stature on the line to condemn the bill as it slithered through parliament. [55]

Elsewhere in Uganda, Canon Gideon Byamugisha was at the forefront of the

---

[54] http://www.bbc.co.uk/news/world-africa-13278374

[55] http://www.huffingtonpost.com/roger-ross-williams/god-loves-uganda_b_3520057.html

opposition in 2009. He is an Anglican priest, active in the fight against HIV/AIDS. At the time of the laws' appearance, Byamugisha made it clear that he believed the law was simply a way of scapegoating an oppressed minority to mask the failings of the government.

He felt obligated to speak out against the crowd, telling the *Guardian* "I realize that if I am happy to speak out against discrimination and stigma in relation to HIV, then I should also be happy to speak out against paralyzing homophobia, sexism, tribalism, puritanism, fundamentalism and against anything else that reduces and diminishes our love, care and support for each other as we travel the road of faith and belief."[56]

---

[56] http://www.theguardian.com/katine/2009/dec/04/gideon-byamugisha-homosexuality-bill

6 The Anti-Homosexuality Law

When 2013 arrived, the bill was revived. There was little doubt that Western pressure weighed heavily on the Ugandan MPs. They feared the West would indeed defund Uganda. The political dilemma they faced was that domestic press, social and religious influence was nearly unanimously in favor of the law[57]. Some lawmakers were so afraid to publicly oppose the law that they asked for a closed debating session. Indeed, a poll taken in 2013, revealed that 96% of the country believed homosexuality was unacceptable.[58]

---

[57]

http://www.observer.ug/index.php?option=com_content&view=article&id=24518:gay-bill-why-mps-fear-open-vote

[58] http://www.pewglobal.org/2013/06/04/the-global-divide-

Despite the moral cowardice of Ugandan lawmakers, Westerners needn't look down their noses. After all, their history is littered with vulgar tactics such as McCarthyism, the destruction of cultures in Africa and the killing of indigenous people. Intolerance is international.

Initially, in the half decade the bill went through, Museveni refused to sign it.

However, he dropped resistance and opened the door to passage in late 2013.[59]

When parliament debated the bill in 2014, only two legislators dared speak against passage.[60] Among all politicians

---

on-homosexuality/

[59] http://www.reuters.com/article/2011/08/23/uganda-gays-idAFL5E7JN1YS20110823

[60]

http://www.nytimes.com/reuters/2014/03/09/world/africa/

in Uganda, the shining star for courage is without doubt Dr. Kizza Besigye, who spoke out strongly before and after the law was passed, saying it was appalling. [61] At 60 years old, a lifetime of opposition to Musevini has made him as tough as steel. His storied life has placed him in jail more than once. [62]

Few politicians stood with him.

When the bill reached the desk of the President, it was all over. On February 24, 2014, Musevini signed the bill that made homosexuality a crime, punishable by life in Uganda's prisons. His likely

---

09reuters-uganda-gays.html?hp

[61] http://www.counterpunch.org/2014/03/07/yoweri-museveni-and-reconstruction-of-homophobic-colonial-legacy-in-africa/#_edn3

[62]http://www.monitor.co.ug/News/National/This-man-Kizza-Besigye--Where-does-he-go-from-here-/-/688334/2086870/-/item/0/-/j4o1fvz/-/index.html

motivation was to drum up support for his re-election bid. As is often the case when a politician of any stripe uses a despised minority to hold onto power, Musevini employed the tactic of portraying Uganda as a victim of international meddling, citing "arrogant and careless Western groups that are fond of coming into our schools and recruiting young children into homosexuality and lesbianism." The theme of outside interference in Ugandan life and culture has been cited repeatedly by the law's proponents.

When the ink was dry, Uganda made a conscious decision to suppress of the rights of gay men and women.

Any homosexual act, even kissing or holding hands, is now illegal.

If you have been legally joined in a same sex marriage, you can be imprisoned. The vague section of the law doesn't specify whether this includes a legal union in another country.

Internet, phones, print, film and any other media are prohibited to "abet" homosexuality. A wide interpretation is available for the courts, again through the murky wording of the law.

Any organization that promotes discussion of homosexuality is illegal.

Finally, extradition power is included in the law. [63]

The Ugandan yellow journal *Red Pepper* wasted little time in becoming one with the state. Within hours of the law's

---

[63]

http://wp.patheos.com.s3.amazonaws.com/blogs/warrenthr ockmorton/files/2014/02/Anti-Homosexuality-Act-2014.pdf passage, it published articles including names of people "accused" of being homosexuals. The death threats to the named came quickly. [64]

Inside of Uganda, the gay community lives in terror. One of the bravest activists, Pepe Julian Onziema, claimed that many of the people in Uganda's gay population are trying to get out of the country.

Ugandan prisons are Stone Age structures. Hard labor, slavery and lack of medical care, provisions and utilities make British and American prisons look like 5 star hotels.[65] Overcrowded and

---

[64]

http://www.nytimes.com/reuters/2014/03/09/world/africa/09reuters-uganda-gays.html?hp

[65] http://www.hrw.org/news/2011/07/14/uganda-forced-labor-disease-imperil-prisoners

disease ridden, as many as half of Uganda's prison population hasn't been to trial.[66]

An indeterminable number of men and women have fled the various places in Africa that have passed these laws. Unfortunately, the refugees find that they aren't welcome, even in countries where no such laws exist.[67]

---

[66] http://www.hrw.org/news/2011/07/14/hard-life-ugandan-prisons

[67] http://www.pambazuka.org/en/category/features/90729

7 Facts and Propaganda: American and British Involvement in Writing the Law

Like any political issue, the law has been used to paint a broad picture of groups involved. Without question, a few fringe American Evangelicals were among many groups of influential people in conceiving the law. Unfortunately, some American Liberals have used the tiny vocal minority to cast them as examples of *all* Conservative Christians. It is easy to see the irony.

In the United States, some evangelical groups assisted law's passage. In fact, one mega-church was deeply involved in getting it passed.

Far away from Africa, Nevada's Canyon Ridge Church bankrolled the bill. The church's pastor, Kevin Odor, funneled money to the scatological minded Martin Ssempa.[68]

However, many more churches and Christian organizations condemned the law. British Christian Organizations in opposition included Accepting Evangelicals, Changing Attitude, Courage, Ekklesia, Fulcrum, Inclusive Church and the Lesbian and Gay Christian Movement (LGCM). Exodus, an organization that believed homosexuality is a treatable disease, condemned the measure in no uncertain terms. The

---

[68]

http://www.salon.com/2010/07/23/canyon_ridge_responds/

Canadian Evangelical Church also offered opposition[69].

In conducting research for this booklet, I find it appalling that blame is heaped on Reverend Rick Warren for the law, when in fact, he fought starting in December of 2009, to publicly repudiate and isolate Bahati. It is likely that Warren helped delay the passage of the bill for a serious length of time through dialogue with the international Christian community.

Rick Warren did not back this law.

"Last week, the nation of Uganda passed a bad law, which I have publicly opposed for nearly 5 years," Warren wrote in March of 2014. "I still oppose it, but

---

[69] http://www.ekklesia.co.uk/node/10640

rumors persist because lies and errors are never removed from the internet."[70]

Many of the voluminous British and American Left Wing writers I read while researching this booklet believed (accurately) that religious fundamentalism is partly to blame for the law, however, their claims that the result came from American Evangelical Churches *alone* is baseless.[71]

In fact, Evangelicals oppose the law in massive numbers, no matter what religious doctrine they hold. Russell Moore, president of the Southern Baptist Convention's Ethics & Religious Liberty Commission, said he does not know a

---

[70]

http://www.theguardian.com/world/2011/feb/17/wikileaks-cables-gay-rights-uganda

[71] http://www.huffingtonpost.com/roger-ross-williams/god-loves-uganda_b_3520057.html

single Evangelical who agrees with the law.[72]

That is not to say there hasn't been meddling. The bill's earliest legislative sponsor, MP David Bahati, used the jargon of the American Evangelical Right to explain the law.

"Here, we don't recognize homosexuality as a right. We are after the sin, not the sinners. We love them - and we want them to repent and come back. It's not an inborn orientation, it's a behavior learnt - and it can be unlearnt. That's why we are encouraging churches and mosques to continue rehabilitating and counselling these people."[73]

---

[72] http://www.washingtonpost.com/national/religion/us-evangelicals-on-the-defense-over-ugandas-new-anti-homosexuality-act/2014/03/04/e91c3b56-a3e9-11e3-b865-38b254d92063_story.html

[73] http://news.bbc.co.uk/2/hi/8412962.stm

Ugandan Rev Dr Olivia Nassaka Banja, Dean School of Divinity and Theology at Uganda Christian University takes a nuanced view. She states flatly that Fundamentalism is not an African trait. It has been brought in from other cultures.[74]

While there are certainly examples of Evangelical churches supporting the law, an unfair broad brush has been used to blame all of the Christian Right. Casting aspersions on them alone falls short. The truly outlandish antics of the bill's western supporters have come from fanatics and quacks. Despite the fact that many Right Wing Pastors believe that homosexuality is a sin and a choice,

---

[74] http://mobile.monitor.co.ug/Life/-/1055104/1196860/-/format/xhtml/-/35mua5z/-/index.html

they have not supported this bill in large numbers. Lumping all of these people in with the fanatics is unfair. [75]

There is something a bit more than condensing in blaming the American Right for the law. After all, Ugandans can make up their minds without being told what to think. It smacks of paternalism and racism.

Dr John Stackhouse lays out a very good case for not blaming the entire Conservative Christian Community in his review of the documentary film *God Loves Uganda.*[76]

Uganda's Muslims played a role as well.

---

[75]

http://www.cnn.com/2009/WORLD/africa/12/08/uganda.anti.gay.bill/index.html?iref=allsearch

[76] http://www.christianitytoday.com/ct/2013/may-web-only/god-loves-uganda.html?start=4

After passage of the bill, Hajji Nsereko Mutumba of the Uganda Muslim Supreme Council said "It takes a courageous leader to defy all the western powers who have gone as far as threatening to cut off aid to Uganda in case the president signs the anti-gay bill."

This, of course, was one of the government's motives throughout the process. The statements and actions of support from the Islamic community offered credibility to the government and opened the way to greater support for the President.

Mutumba, just hours after the bill was signed, urged Muslims to rally around Museveni. [77]

---

[77] http://www.onislam.net/english/news/africa/469431-uganda-muslims-laud-anti-gay-bill.html

Sheikh Ramathan Shaban Mubajje, a prominent cleric, hoped that the law's enforcement would allow the government to would "round up" gays and "send them to an island to die." [78]

---

[78]

http://www.cnn.com/2009/WORLD/africa/12/08/uganda.anti.gay.bill/index.html?iref=allsearch

8 **Reaction and Reckoning**

Incredibly, at Musevini's raucous post-signing press conference, the Ugandan President clearly and emphatically stated Uganda didn't need western aid. It was an interesting thought when the US and British government discussed the idea of actually cutting the spigot off.[79] His ridiculous claim that an aid cut-off was "blackmail," had been foreseen by Bahati five years earlier and he, the law's author, was prepared to give up aid. Uganda's President should wake up to reality. You can't blackmail anyone with a gift. Gifts are given with friendship and

---

[79] http://www.cnn.com/2014/02/24/world/africa/verjee-uganda-museveni-anti-gay/

common ground, which Uganda now lacks with Western nations.[80]

In the week following the law's passage, international headlines revealed that another newspaper had published a list of "the names of 200" gays. In addition to be a direct tactic of McCarthyism, the roster was practically a hit list.[81]

Dr. Lively, the American troubadour of the anti-gay Right, expressed disappointment with the law, saying it was too harsh.[82]

---

[80] http://harpers.org/archive/2010/09/straight-mans-burden/8/

[81] http://www.counterpunch.org/2014/03/07/yoweri-museveni-and-reconstruction-of-homophobic-colonial-legacy-in-africa/

[82]

http://www.oregonlive.com/mapes/index.ssf/2014/02/scott_lively_former_oregon_ant.html

American and British governments spoke out quickly and forcefully against the measure. British High Commission officials communicated a desire for Uganda to add a constitutional clause protecting the rights of Gays. The idea was ignored.

President Obama's disapproval of the law was brought up in the Ugandan leader's February 25th press conference by a western reporter. Museveni replied that this was our [Uganda's] country and it would be run the way Uganda saw fit. He said the west was guilty of hypocrisy since Uganda didn't impose its social beliefs on the United States, hinting that the American family was decadent.[83] The remark played well to the Ugandans in

---

[83] http://edition.cnn.com/2014/02/24/world/africa/uganda-anti-gay-bill/

the room. [84] United States Secretary of State John Kerry correctly compared passage of the law to the Nuremberg laws against Jews in the years before World War II erupted. [85] In fact, gays were rounded up and killed in the Holocaust due to 1935 Nazi Nuremberg Laws.[86]

John Kerry added "...we are beginning an internal review of our relationship with the government of Uganda to ensure that all dimensions of our engagement, including assistance programs, uphold our anti-discrimination policies and

---

[84] Uganda's President Museveni signs controversial anti-gay bill into law

[85] http://www.bbc.com/news/world-africa-26378230

[86] Richard Plant's, *The Pink Triangle: The Nazi War Against Homosexuals*

principles and reflect our values,"
signaling that US aid may come.[87]

What complicates the West's response is
Ugandan support in fighting Islamists in
Africa. The government gathers
information and supplies troops readily in
combating Jihad. If the West defunds
Uganda and loses it as an ally, the
missing help could be significant. [88]

Speaking for Britain, Foreign Secretary
William Hague condemned what the
Ugandans had done on February 25. It
was a strong rebuke, but it included no
actual consequences for the bigotry of
the law. Additionally, the High

---

[87] http://www.theeastafrican.co.ke/news/Norway-cuts--8-
3m-aid-to-Uganda-over-anti-gay-law/-/2558/2222782/-
/dewf1f/-/index.html

[88]

http://www.nytimes.com/reuters/2014/03/09/world/africa/
09reuters-uganda-gays.html?hp

Commissioner for Ugandan relations co-signed a statement with 16 other representatives to condemn the law a few days later. [89] David Cameron has indicated, along with President Obama, that aid to Uganda might be completely cut off. [90]

On the 25th, Denmark led the way by pulling foreign aid to Uganda's court system immediately.

The same day, Canadian Foreign Minister David Baird said 'Canada is extremely disappointed that President Museveni has signed this piece of legislation, which will make homosexuality punishable with life imprisonment. We strongly urge the

---

[89]https://www.gov.uk/government/news/foreign-secretary-saddened-and-disappointed-by-ugandan-anti-homosexuality-law

[90] http://www.onislam.net/english/news/africa/469431-uganda-muslims-laud-anti-gay-bill.html

President to protect the human rights of all Ugandans regardless of their sexual orientation, in accordance with Uganda's constitution" [91]

One day later, Norway cut 8 million dollars from Uganda.

On the 28th, the World Bank stopped the payment of a $90m (£54m) loan. Uganda reacted swiftly calling the action blackmail. This was a near complete revision of the government's initial attitude that what went on in Uganda was Uganda's business. [92] Jim Young Yim, the World Bank's president wrote about the devastating effects discriminatory laws have on economies

---

[91] http://www.gaystarnews.com/article/first-countries-cut-aid-ugandan-government-over-anti-gay-law250214

[92] http://www.bbc.com/news/world-africa-26378230

in an editorial in the Washington Post.[93] Along with the World Bank, Sweden, Norway, Denmark and the Netherlands have ended or suspended aid to Uganda.[94]

Russia alone has used the law to ally itself with Uganda. None other than the tyrant Vladimir Putin was soon working to establish ties with Uganda in a state visit in late 2012. Like a scorned lover, Musevini waved around Putin's "help" as an example of Uganda's "independence."[95]

---

[93]http://www.washingtonpost.com/opinions/jim-yong-kim-the-high-costs-of-institutional-discrimination/2014/02/27/8cd37ad0-9fc5-11e3-b8d8-94577ff66b28_story.html

[94]

http://www.nytimes.com/reuters/2014/03/09/world/africa/09reuters-uganda-gays.html?hp

[95]

http://www.oregonlive.com/mapes/index.ssf/2014/02/scott_

On March 7, Sweden dropped the hammer and cut off much of its' aid to the Ugandan Government. "Swedish aid is not unconditional. The Government is therefore now choosing to suspend government-to-government payments still due under our current strategy for Uganda, with the exception of research cooperation," said Hillevi Engström, representing Swedish diplomats.

The move cost Uganda roughly 1 million US Dollars.

Combined with the World Bank, Denmark and Norway, the loss of vital aid to Uganda is 110 million US Dollars.[96]

---

lively_former_oregon_ant.html

[96]http://www.aljazeera.com/news/africa/2014/03/sweden-suspends-uganda-aid-over-anti-gay-law-20143661242394264.html

With a generous annual foreign aid package of $500 million dollars to Uganda, the United States, should it choose to do so, holds the best hand at compelling Uganda to repeal or amend the law.[97] If those funds are taken away, the Ugandan economy will eventually collapse. [98]

The boasts made by Ugandan leaders going without international aid are already being tested.

The Ugandan shilling is losing value. It has lost 3% since the law's passage.[99]

The one trick pony economy of Uganda has a GDP of 20 billion dollars. The loss

---

[97]http://www.bloombergview.com/articles/2011-10-27/why-uganda-s-anti-gay-legislation-is-the-world-s-business-view

[99]http://www.bloomberg.com/news/2014-02-26/uganda-s-anti-gay-law-punished-in-foreign-exchange-market.html

of nearly a billion US dollars would be bad enough. The down year for coffee that will arrive eventually through nature's law would then destroy Uganda. They might be the next Zimbabwe, which is marveled at as the ultimate example of a hyper-inflated economy.[100]

Corporations and Companies in the West are formulating a response. [101]

When one group's rights are taken away in any part of our modern world, the whole nation will pay the consequences.

Dark days loom for Uganda.

---

[100]http://www.bloomberg.com/news/2014-02-26/uganda-s-anti-gay-law-punished-in-foreign-exchange-market.html

[101]

http://www.nytimes.com/reuters/2014/03/09/world/africa/09reuters-uganda-gays.html?hp

~Appendix~

THE ANTI-HOMOSEXUALITY ACT, 2014.

ARRANGEMENT OF SECTIONS.

PART I—PRELIMINARY.

Section

1. Interpretation.

PART II—PROHIBITION OF HOMOSEXUALITY.

2. The offence of homosexuality.
3. Aggravated homosexuality.
4. Attempt to commit homosexuality.
5. Protection, assistance and payment of compensation to
victims of homosexuality.
6. Confidentiality.

PART III—RELATED OFFENCES AND PENALTIES.

7. Aiding and abetting homosexuality.
8. Conspiracy to engage in homosexuality.
9. Procuring homosexuality by threats, etc.
10. Detention with intent to commit homosexuality.
11. Brothels.
12. Same sex marriage.
13. Promotion of homosexuality.

PART IV—MISCELLANEOUS PROVISIONS.

14. Extradition.
15. Regulations.

Schedule

Currency point.

1

Act *Anti-Homosexuality Act* **2014**
2
Act *Anti-Homosexuality Act* **2014**
THE ANTI-HOMOSEXUALITY ACT, 2014.
An Act to prohibit any form of sexual relations between persons
of the same sex; prohibit the promotion or recognition of such
relations and to provide for other related matters.
DATE OF ASSENT:
Date of Commencement:
BE IT ENACTED by Parliament as follows:
PART I—PRELIMINARY.
1. Interpretation.
In this Act, unless the context otherwise requires—
"authority" means having power and control over other people
because of your knowledge and official position; and shall
include a person who exercises religious, political,
economic or social authority;
"child" means a person below the age of eighteen years;
"court" means a chief magistrates court;
"currency point" has the value assigned to it in the Schedule to
this Act;
3
Act *Anti-Homosexuality Act* **2014**
"disability" means a substantial limitation of daily life activities

caused by physical, mental or sensory impairment and
environment barriers resulting in limited participation;
"felony" means an offence which is declared by law to be a
felony or if not declared to be a misdemeanor is punishable
without proof of previous conviction, with death or with
imprisonment for three years or more;
"HIV" means the Human Immunodeficiency Virus;
"homosexual" means a person who engages or attempts to
engage in same gender sexual activity;
"homosexuality" means same gender or same sex sexual acts;
"Minister" means the Minister responsible for ethics and
integrity;
"misdemeanor" means any offence which is not a felony;
"serial offender" means a person who has previous convictions
of the offence of homosexuality or related offences;
"sexual act" includes—
(a) physical sexual activity that does not necessarily
culminate in intercourse and may include the touching
of another's breast, vagina, penis or anus;

(b) stimulation or penetration of a vagina or mouth or
anus or any part of the body of any person, however
slight by a sexual organ;
(c) the unlawful use of any object or organ by a person on
another person's sexual organ or anus or mouth;
"sexual organ" means a vagina, penis or any artificial sexual
contraption;
"touching" includes touching—
4

Act *Anti-Homosexuality Act* **2014**

(a) with any part of the body;
(b) with anything else;
(c) through anything;
and in particular includes touching amounting to
penetration of any sexual organ, anus or mouth.
"victim" includes a person who is involved in homosexual
activities against his or her will.
PART II—HOMOSEXUALITY AND RELATED PRACTICES.

2. The offence of homosexuality.

(1) A person commits the offence of homosexuality if—
(a) he penetrates the anus or mouth of another person of the
same sex with his penis or any other sexual contraption;

(b) he or she uses any object or sexual contraption to penetrate
or stimulate sexual organ of a person of the same sex;
(c) he or she touches another person with the intention of
committing the act of homosexuality.
(2) A person who commits an offence under this section shall be
liable, on conviction, to imprisonment for life.

3. Aggravated homosexuality.

(1) A person commits the offence of aggravated homosexuality
where the—
(a) person against whom the offence is committed is below the
age of eighteen years;
(b) offender is a person living with HIV;
5

Act *Anti-Homosexuality Act* **2014**

(c) offender is a parent or guardian of the person against whom
the offence is committed;
(d) offender is a person in authority over the person against
whom the offence is committed;
(e) victim of the offence is a person with disability;
(f) offender is a serial offender; or
(g) offender applies, administers or causes to be used by any
man or woman any drug, matter or thing with intent to

stupefy or overpower him or her so as to enable any person
to have unlawful carnal connection with any person of the
same sex.

(2) A person who commits the offence of aggravated
homosexuality shall be liable, on conviction, to imprisonment for life.

(3) Where a person is charged with the offence under this
section, that person shall undergo a medical examination to ascertain
his or her HIV status.

4. Attempt to commit homosexuality.

(1) A person who attempts to commit the offence of
homosexuality commits a felony and is liable, on conviction, to
imprisonment for seven years.

(2) A person who attempts to commit the offence of aggravated
homosexuality commits an offense and is liable, on conviction, to
imprisonment for life.

5. Protection, assistance and payment of compensation to
victims of homosexuality.

(1) A victim of homosexuality shall not be penalized for any
crime committed as a direct result of his or her involvement in
homosexuality.

6

Act *Anti-Homosexuality Act* **2014**

(2) A victim of homosexuality shall be assisted to enable his or
her views and concerns to be presented and considered at the
appropriate stages of the criminal proceedings.

(3) Where a person is convicted of homosexuality or aggravated
homosexuality under sections 2 and 3 of this Act, the court may, in
addition to any sentence imposed on the offender, order that the
victim of the offence be paid compensation by the offender for any
physical, sexual or psychological harm caused to the victim by the
offence.

(4) The amount of compensation shall be determined by the
court and the court shall take into account the extent of harm suffered
by the victim of the offence, the degree of force used by the offender
and medical and other expenses incurred by the victim as a result of
the offence.

6. Confidentiality.

(1) At any stage of the investigation or trial of an offence under
this Act, law enforcement officer, prosecutor, judicial officer and
medical practitioner, and any party to the case, shall recognize the

right to privacy of the victim.

(2) For the purpose of subsection (1), in cases involving children
and other cases where the court considers it appropriate, proceedings
of the court shall be conducted in camera.

(3) Any editor, publisher, reporter or columnist in case of printed
materials, announcer or producer in case of television and radio,
producer or director of a film in case of the movie industry, or any
person utilizing trimedia facilities or information technology who
publishes or causes the publicity of the names and personal
circumstances or any other information tending to establish the
victim's identity without authority of the victim or court, commits an
offence and is liable, on conviction, to a fine not exceeding two
hundred and fifty currency points.

7

Act *Anti-Homosexuality Act* **2014**

PART III—RELATED OFFENCES AND PENALTIES.

7. Aiding and abetting homosexuality.

A person who aids, abets, counsels or procures another to engage in
acts of homosexuality commits an offence and is liable, on
conviction, to imprisonment for seven years.

8. Conspiracy to engage in homosexuality.

A person who conspires with another to induce another person of the
same sex by any means of false pretence or other fraudulent means to
permit any person of the same sex to have unlawful carnal knowledge
of him or her commits an offence and is liable, on conviction, to
imprisonment for seven years.

9. Procuring homosexuality by threats.

(1) A person who—

(a) by threats or intimidation procures or attempts to procure any
woman or man to have any unlawful carnal knowledge with
any person of the same sex; or

(b) by false pretences or false representations procures any
woman or man to have any unlawful carnal connection with
any person of the same sex;

commits an offence and is liable on conviction to imprisonment for
seven years

(2) A person shall not be convicted of an offence under this section
upon the evidence of one witness only, unless that witness is corroborated
in some material particular by evidence implicating the accused.

10. Detention with intent to commit homosexuality.

A person who detains another person with the intention to commit
acts of homosexuality with him or her or with any other person
commits an offence and is liable, on conviction, to imprisonment for
seven years.

8

Act *Anti-Homosexuality Act* **2014**

11. Brothels.

(1) A person who keeps a house, room, set of rooms or place of
any kind for purposes of homosexuality commits an offence and is
liable, on conviction, to imprisonment for seven years.

(2) A person being the owner or occupier of premises or having or
acting or assisting in the management or control of the premises, induces
or knowingly suffers any man or woman to resort to or be upon such
premises for the purpose of being unlawfully and carnally known by any
man or woman of the same sex whether such carnal knowledge is
intended to be with any particular man or woman generally, commits a
felony and is liable, on conviction, to imprisonment for five years.

12. Same sex marriage.

(1) A person who purports to contract a marriage with another

person of the same sex commits the offence of homosexuality and
shall be liable, on conviction, to imprisonment for life.

(2) A person or institution commits an offence if that person or
institution conducts a marriage ceremony between persons of the
same sex and shall, on conviction, be liable to imprisonment for a
maximum of seven years for individuals or cancellation of licence for
an institution.

13. Promotion of homosexuality.

(1) A person who—

(a) participates in production, procuring, marketing,
broadcasting, disseminating, publishing of pornographic
materials for purposes of promoting homosexuality;

(b) funds or sponsors homosexuality or other related activities;

(c) offers premises and other related fixed or movable assets for
purposes of homosexuality or promoting homosexuality;

(d) uses electronic devices which include internet, films,
mobile phones for purposes of homosexuality or promoting
homosexuality; or

9

Act *Anti-Homosexuality Act* **2014**

(e) who acts as an accomplice or attempts to promote or in any
way abets homosexuality and related practices;
commits an offence and is liable, on conviction, to a fine of five
thousand currency points or imprisonment of a minimum of five
years and a maximum of seven years or both fine and imprisonment.

(2) Where the offender is a corporate body or a business or an
association or a non-governmental organization, on conviction its
certificate of registration shall be cancelled and the director, proprietor or
promoter shall be liable, on conviction, to imprisonment for seven years.

PART IV—MISCELLANEOUS.

14. Extradition.

A person charged with an offence under this Act shall be liable to
extradition under the existing extradition laws.

15. Regulations.

The Minister may, by statutory instrument, make regulations
generally for better carrying out the provisions of this Act.

10

Act *Anti-Homosexuality Act* **2014**

SCHEDULE

s.1.

CURRENCY POINT

One currency point is equivalent to twenty thousand shillings.

11

Act *Anti-Homosexuality Act* **2014**[102]

---

[102]

http://wp.patheos.com.s3.amazonaws.com/blogs/warrenthr ockmorton/files/2014/02/Anti-Homosexuality-Act-2014.pdf

www.ingramcontent.com/pod-product-compliance
Lightning Source LLC
Chambersburg PA
CBHW060201290526
45789CB00003B/1113